WELCOME
TO
COLOR ME BOTANICALS V
- AN ADULT COLORING BOOK -

ISBN: 1522944680
ISBN-13: 978-1522944683

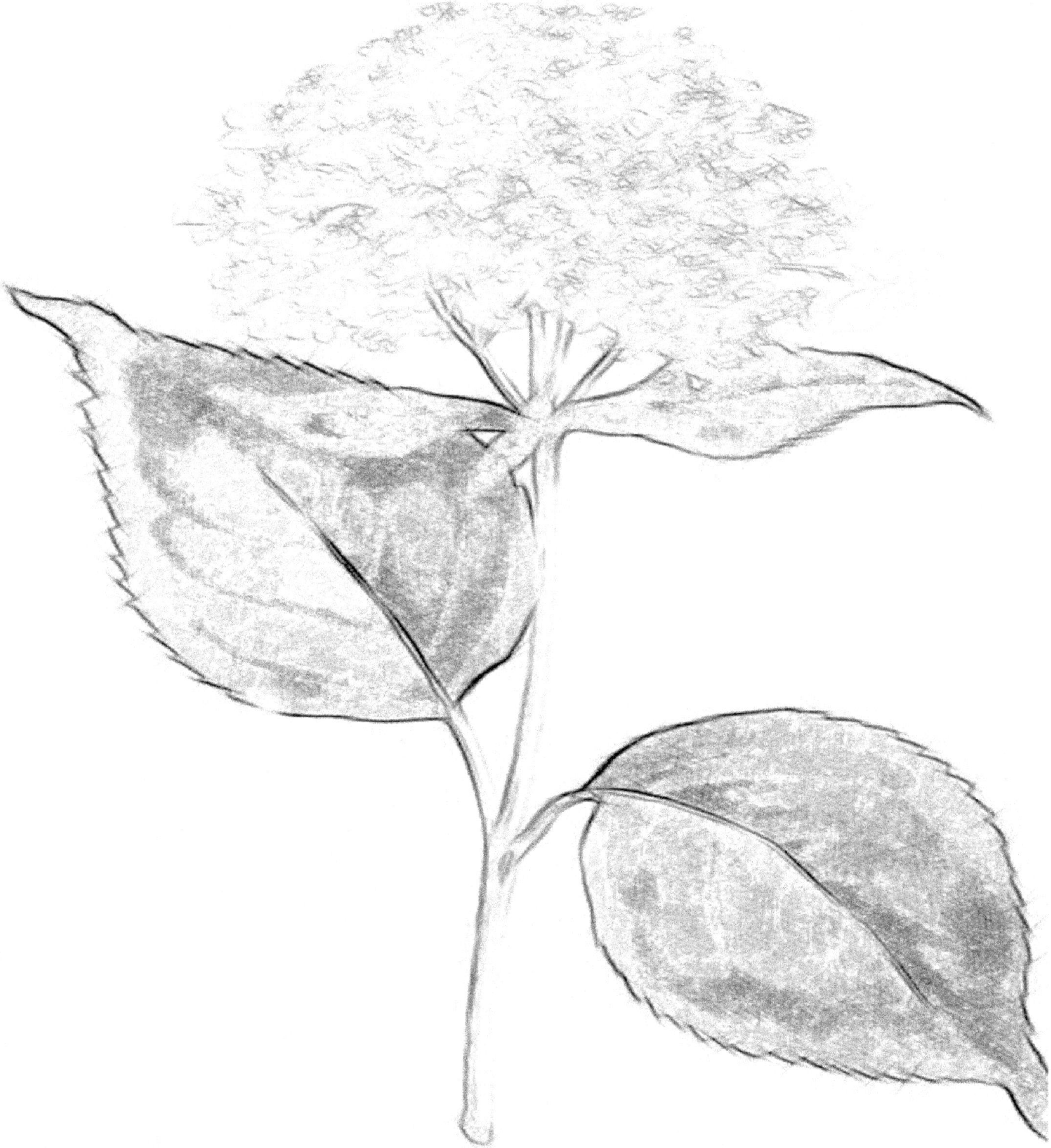

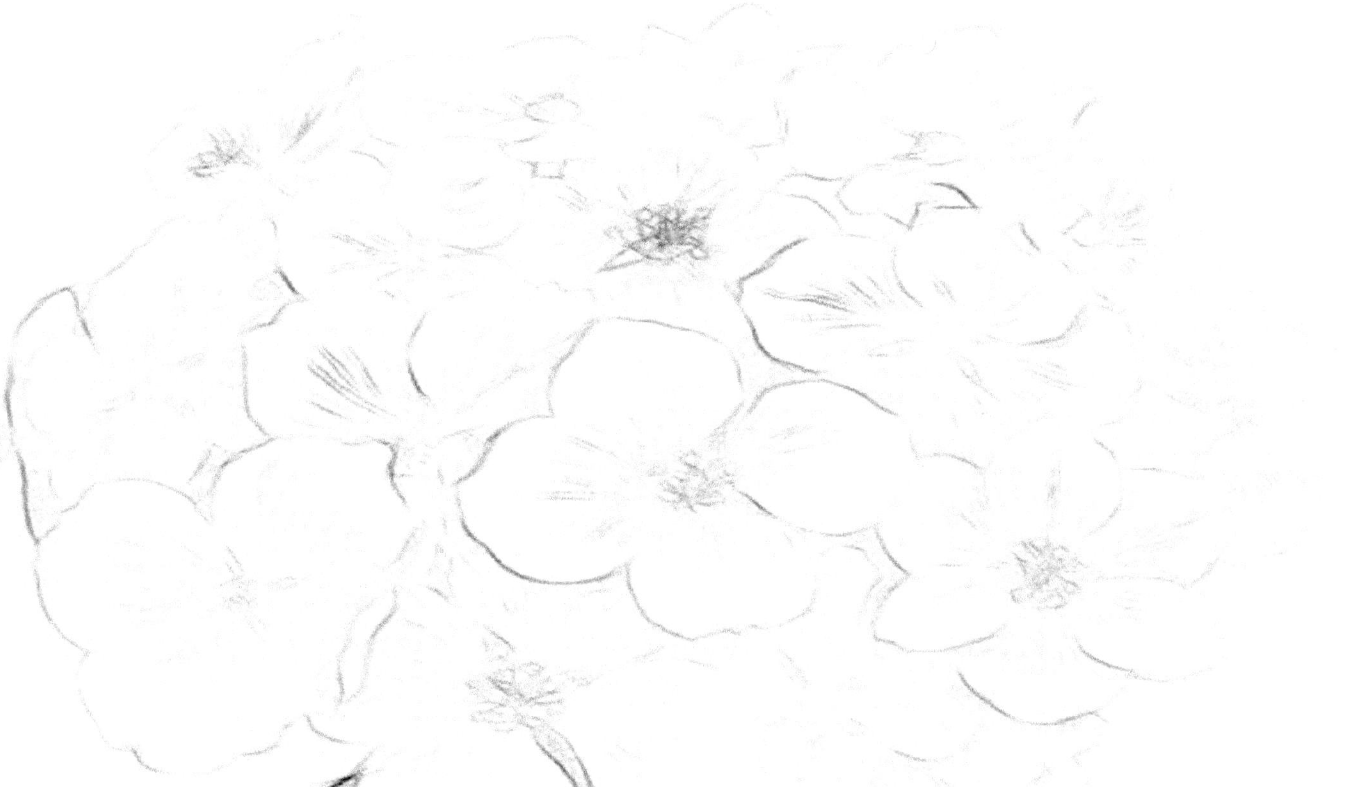

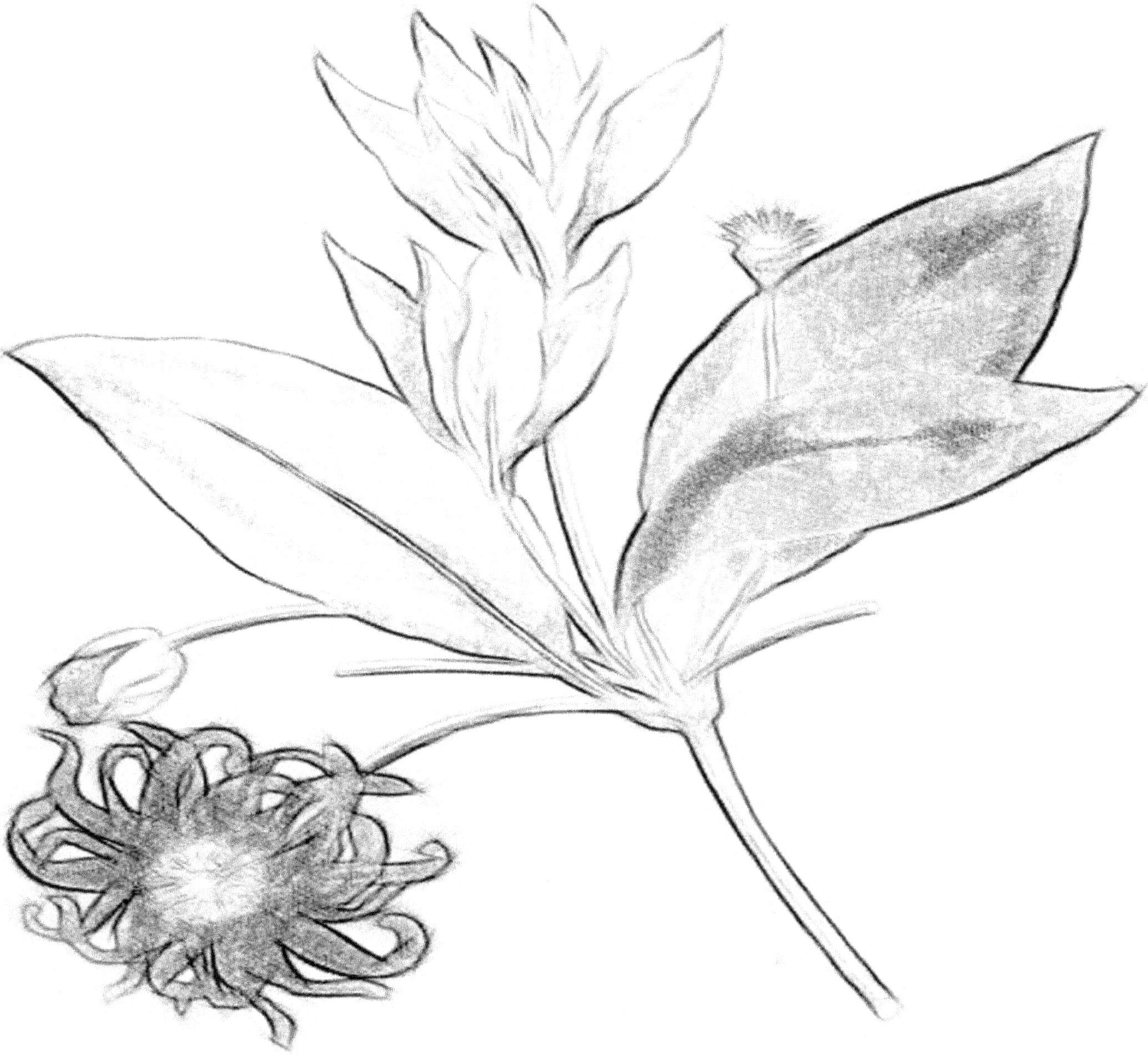

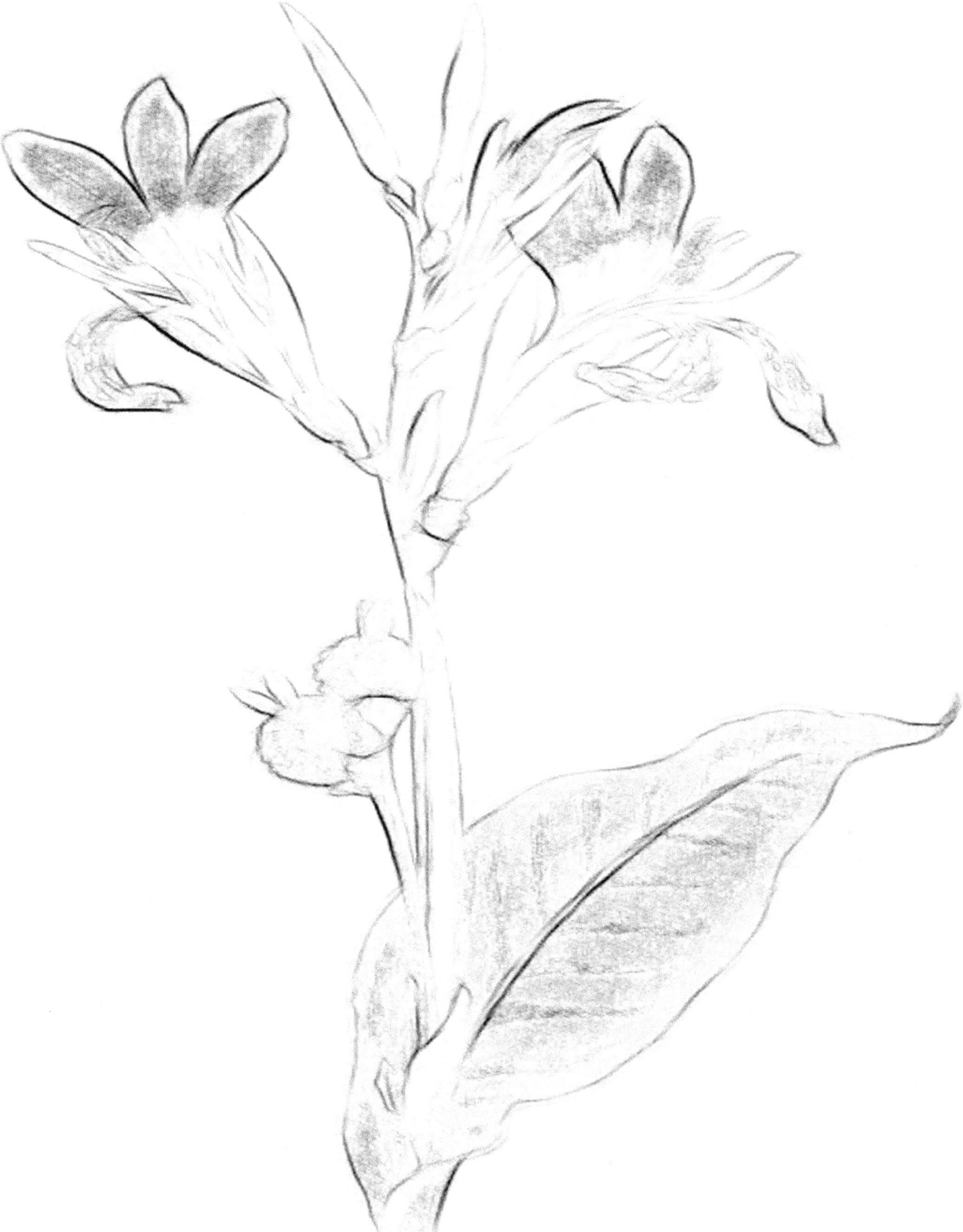

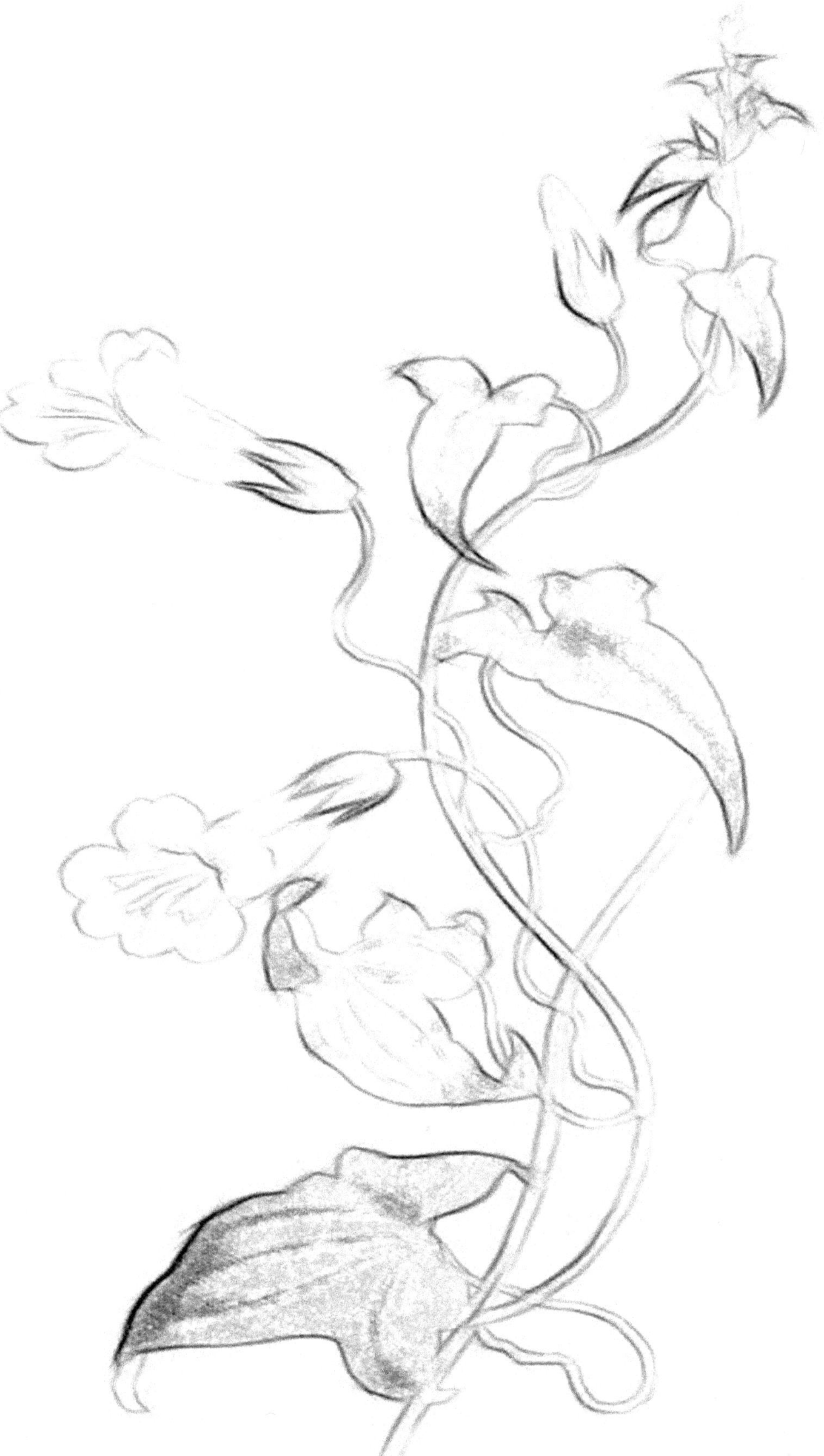

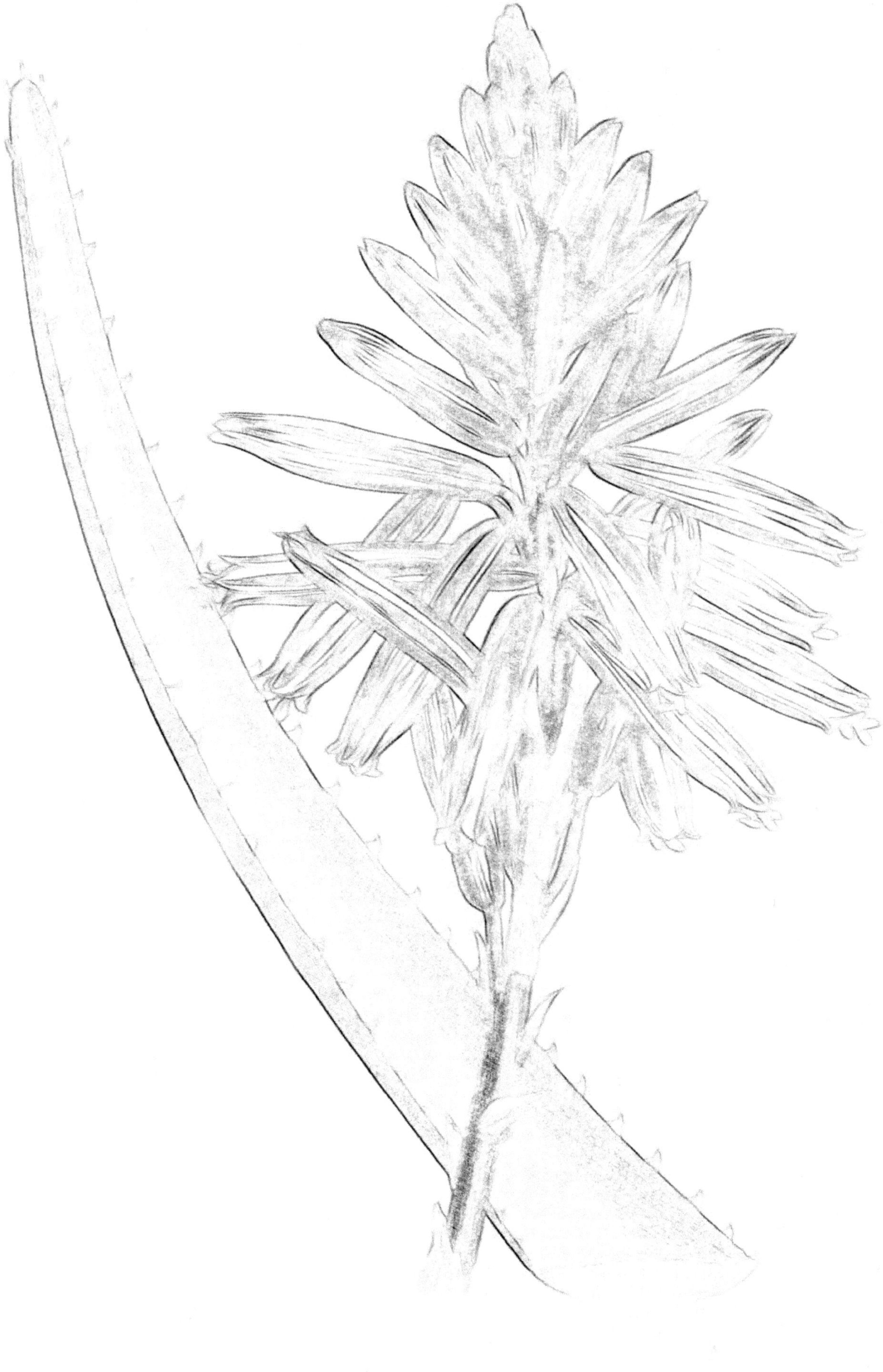

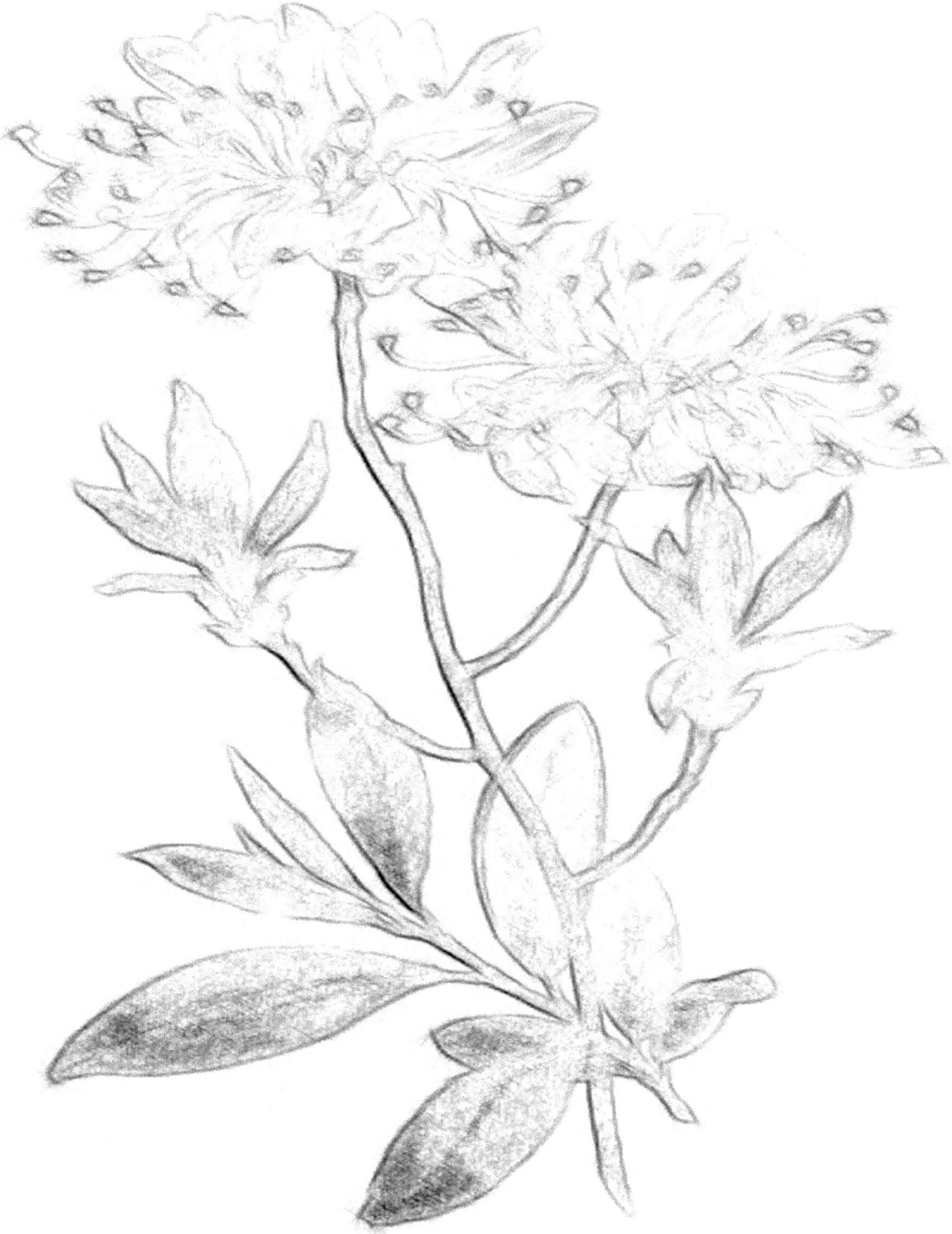

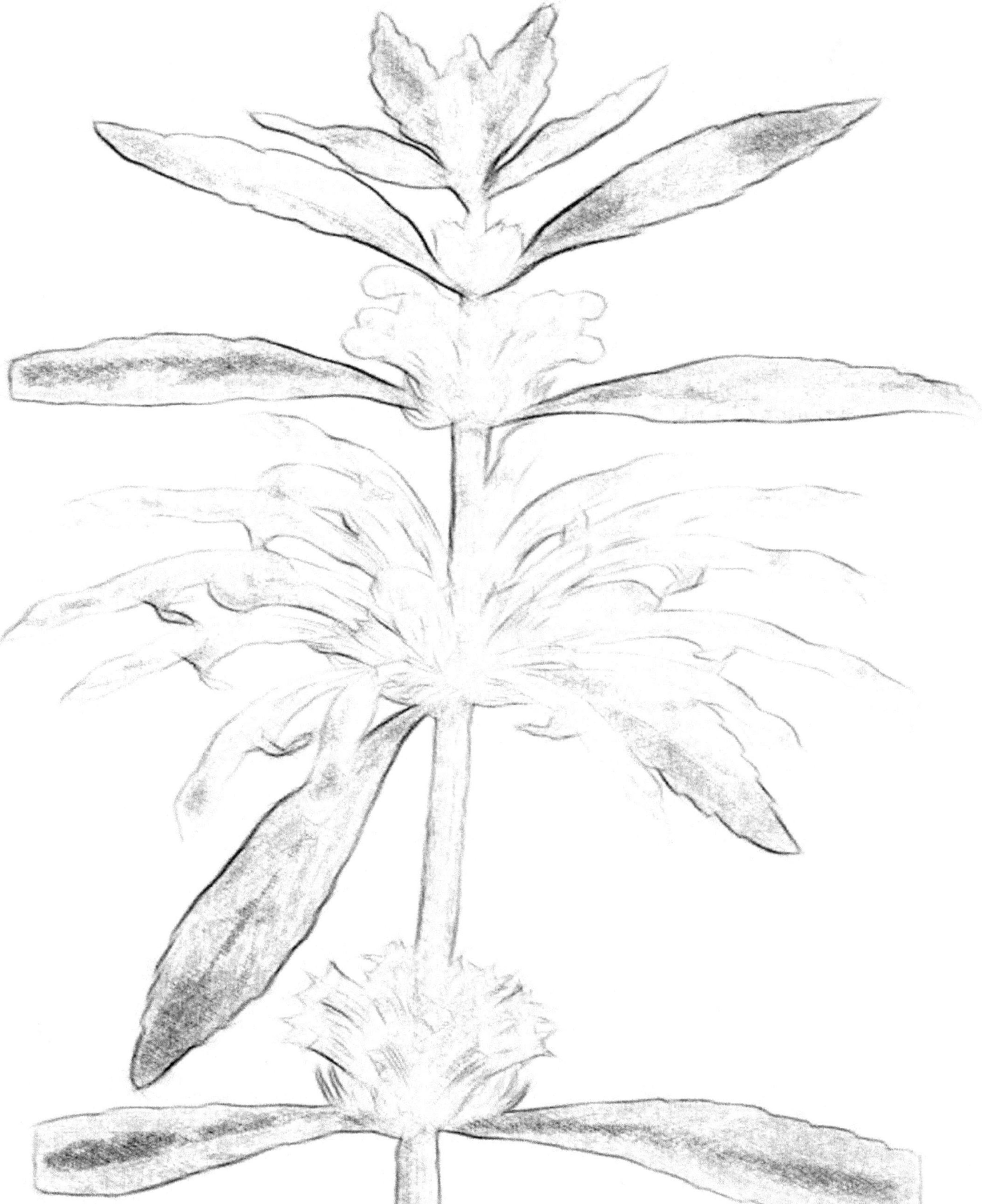

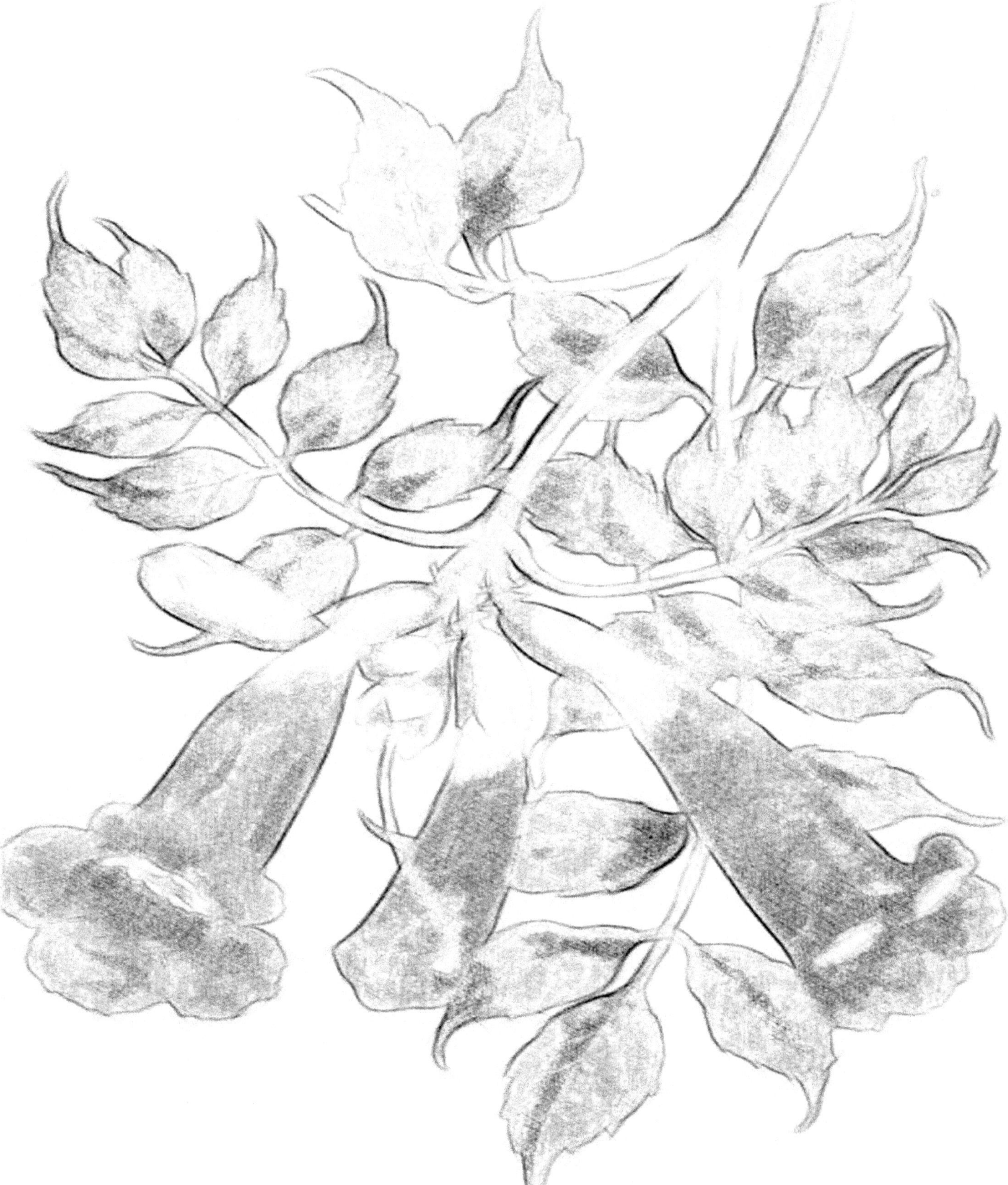

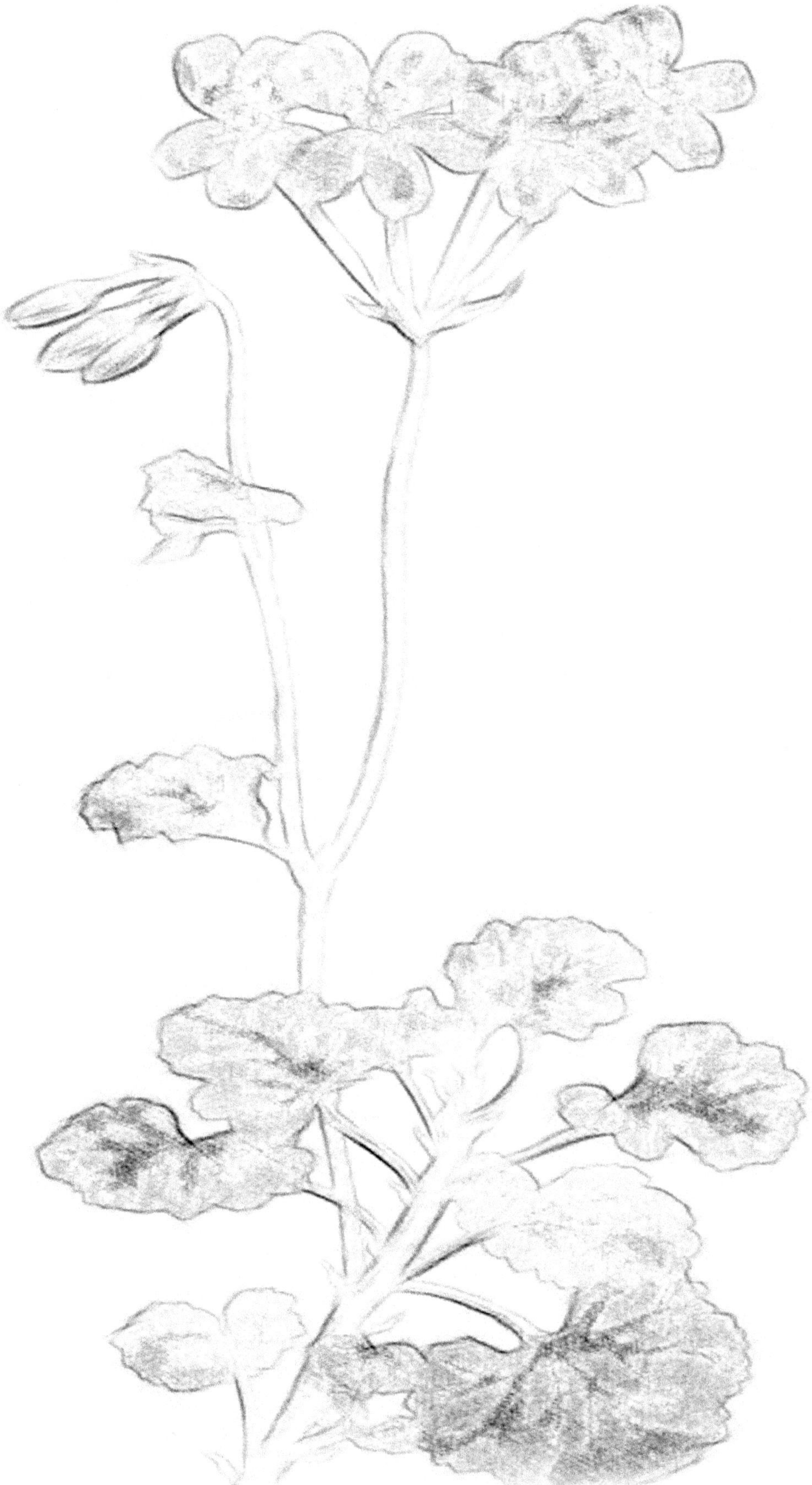

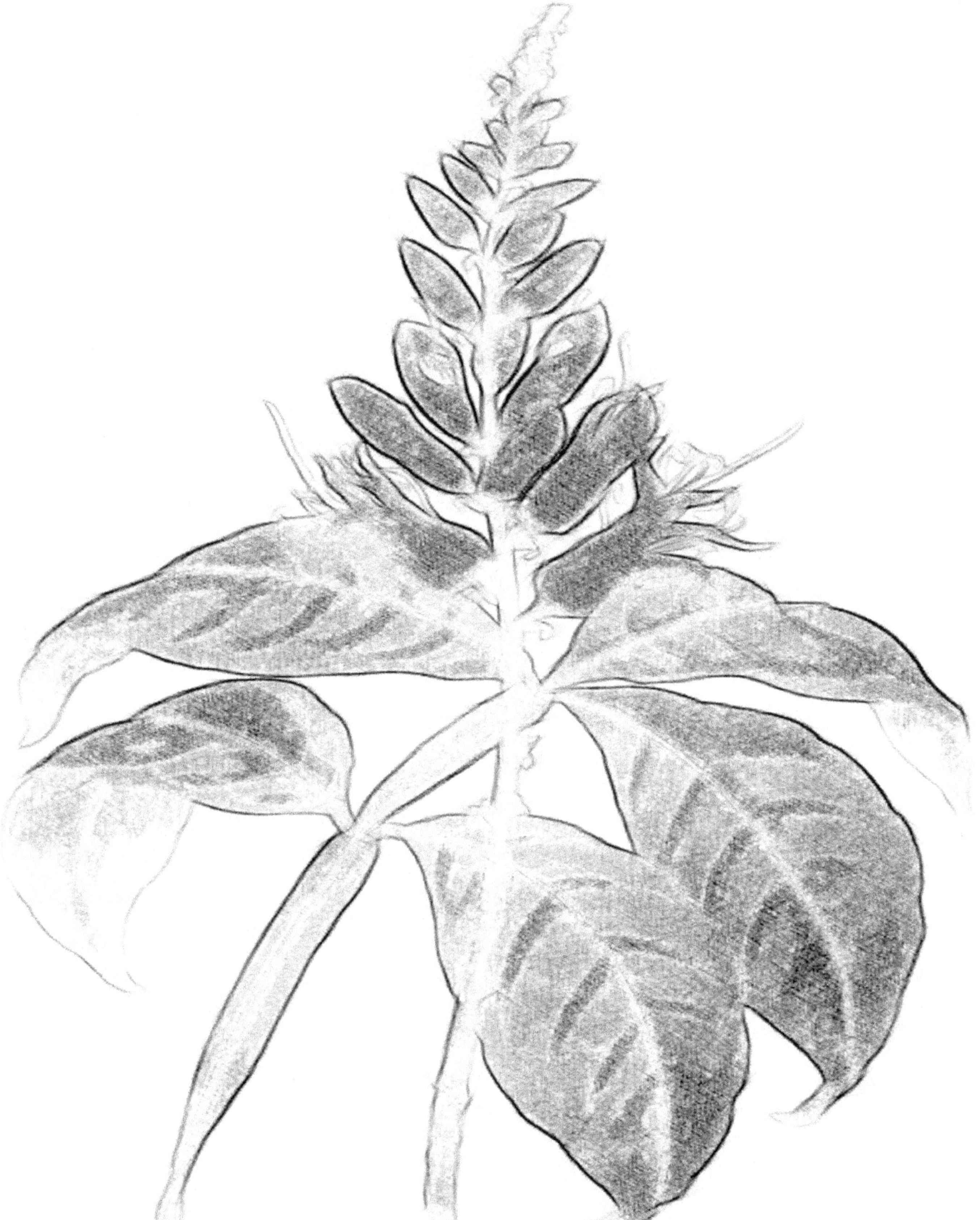

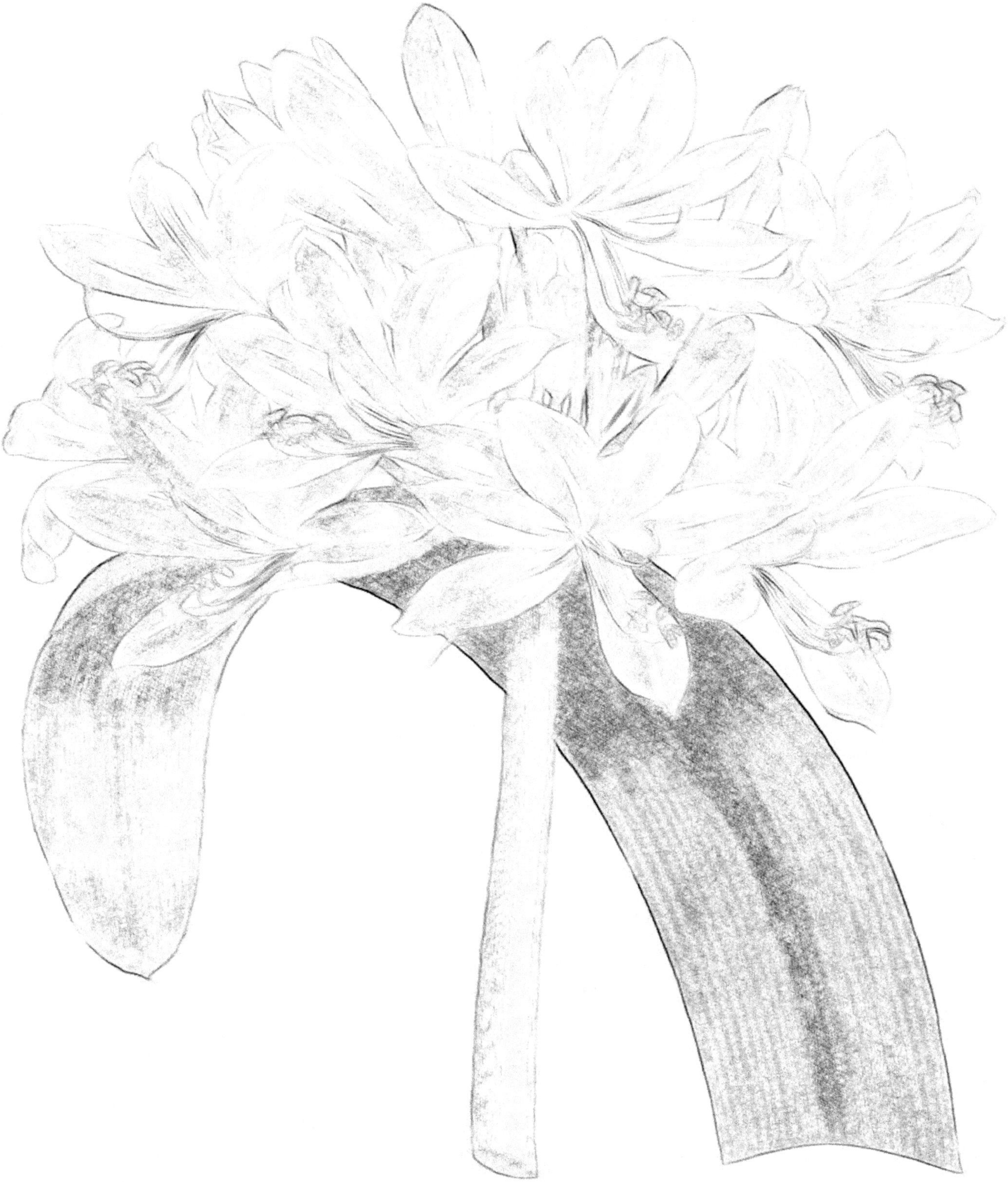

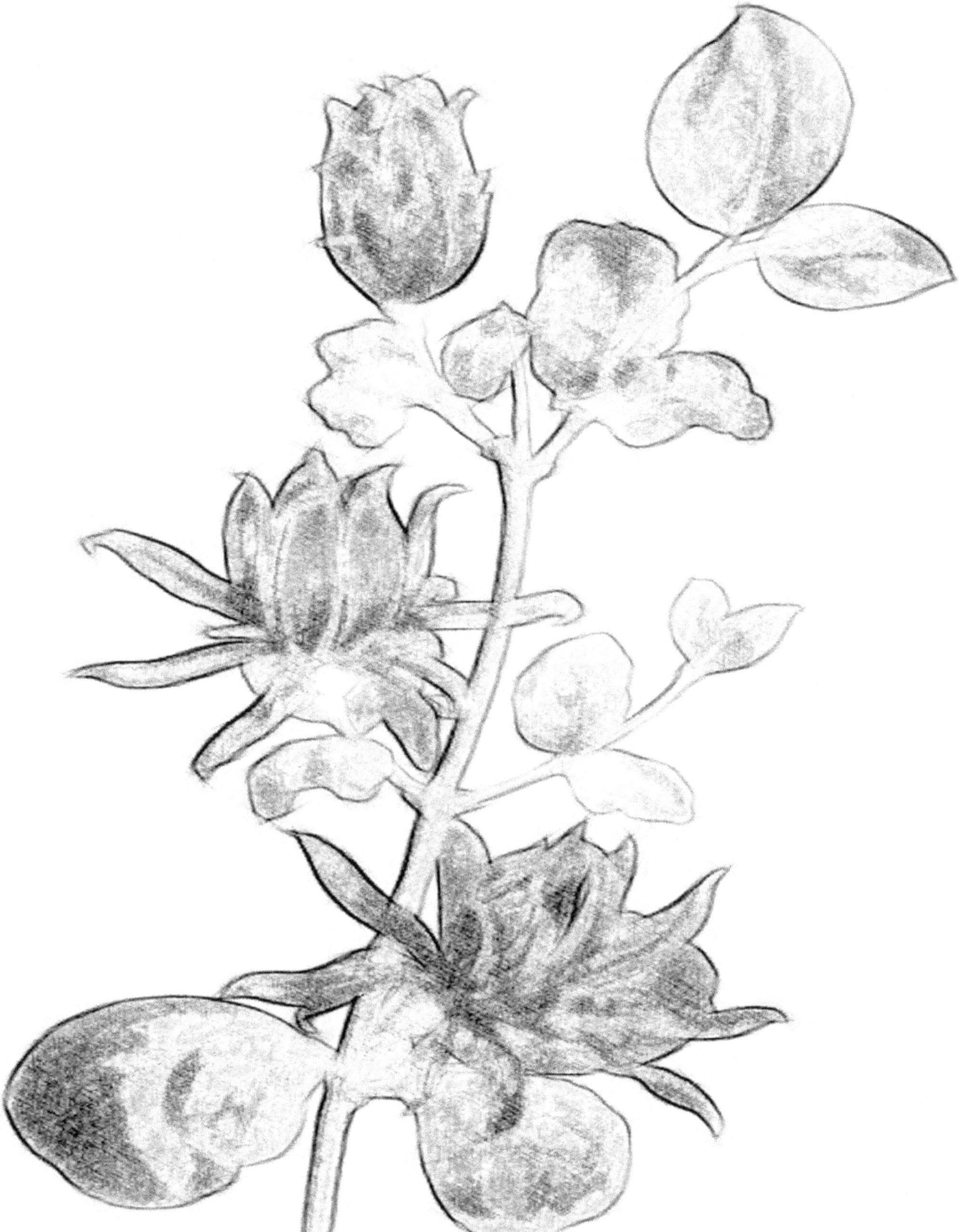

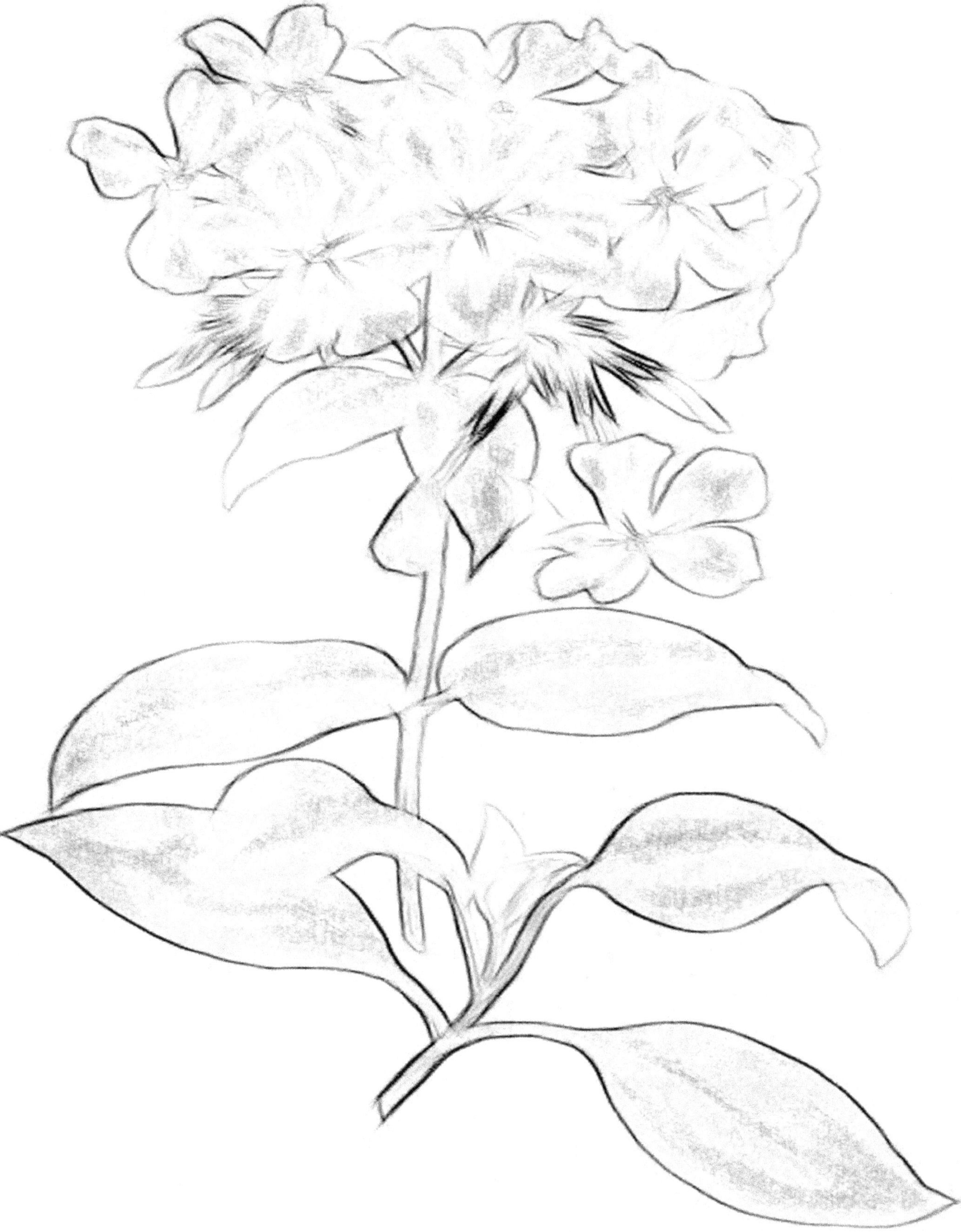

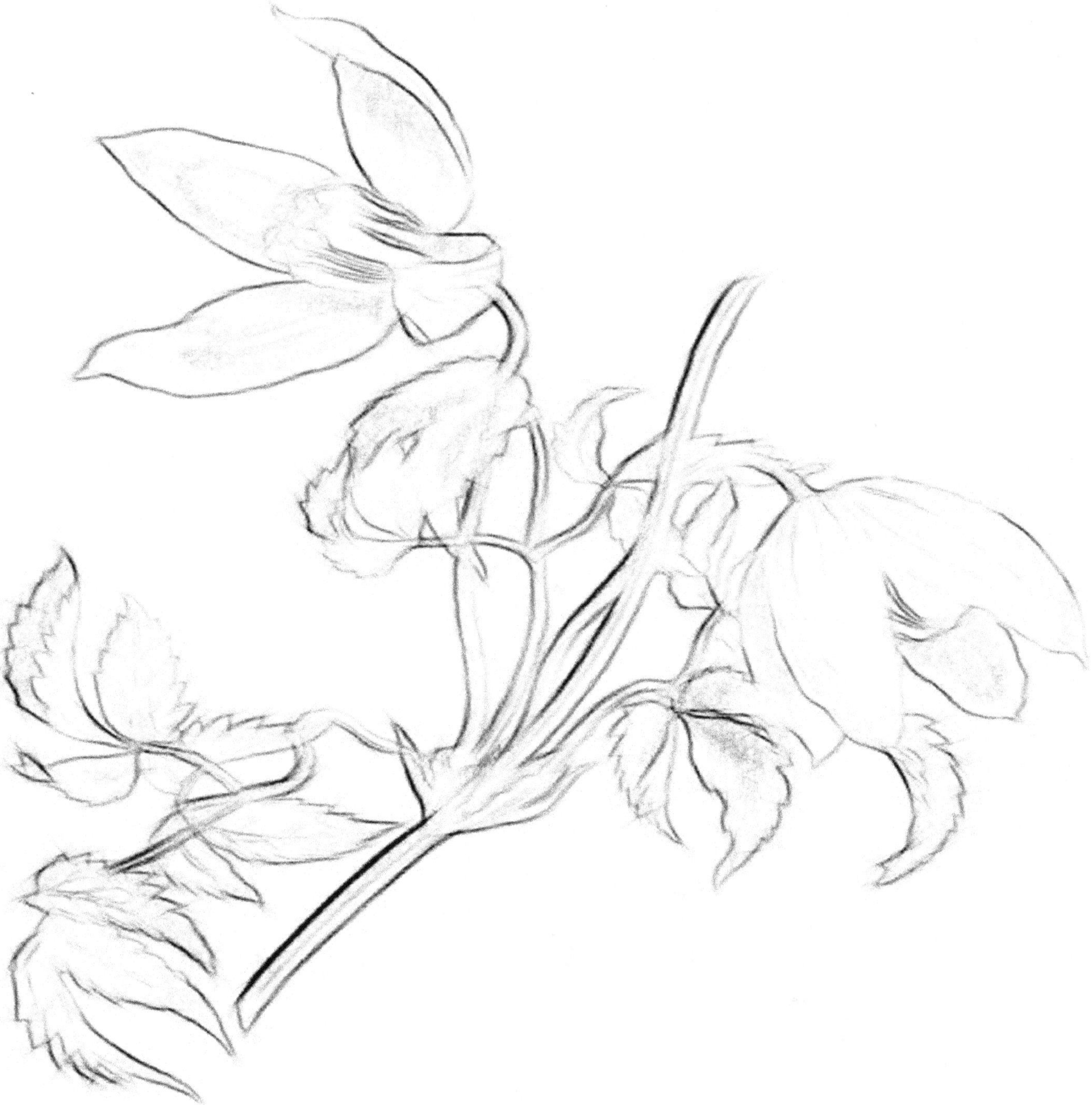

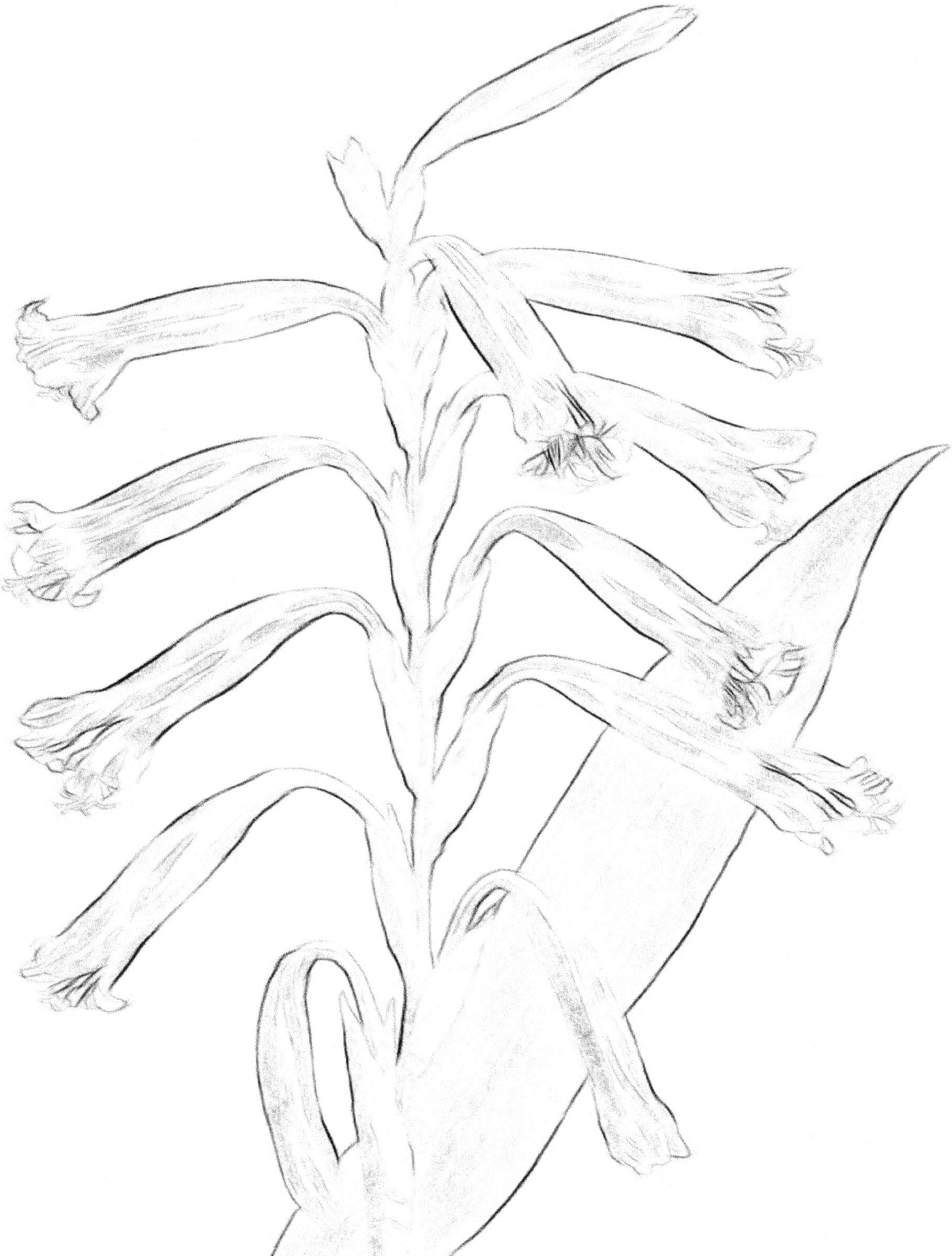

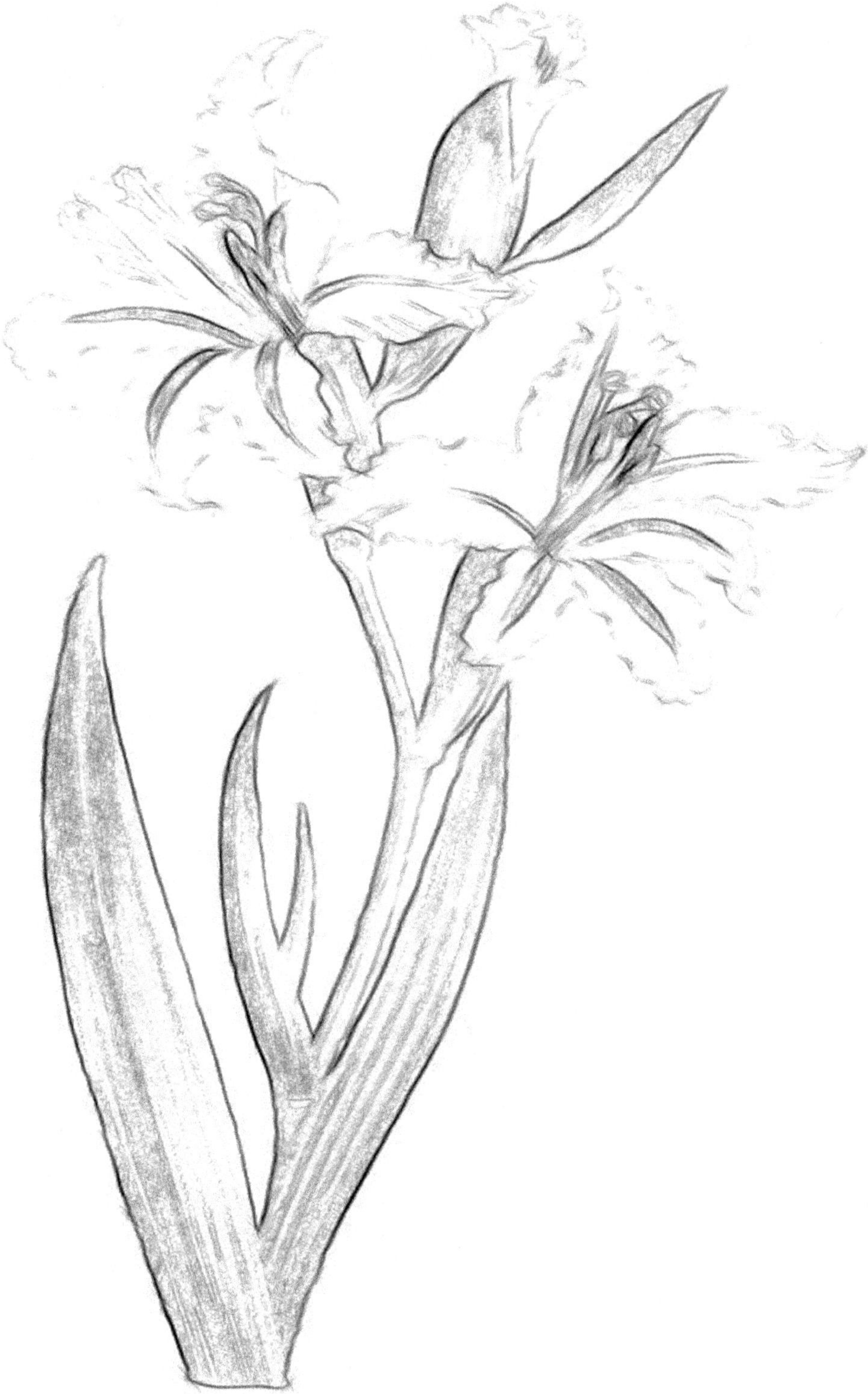

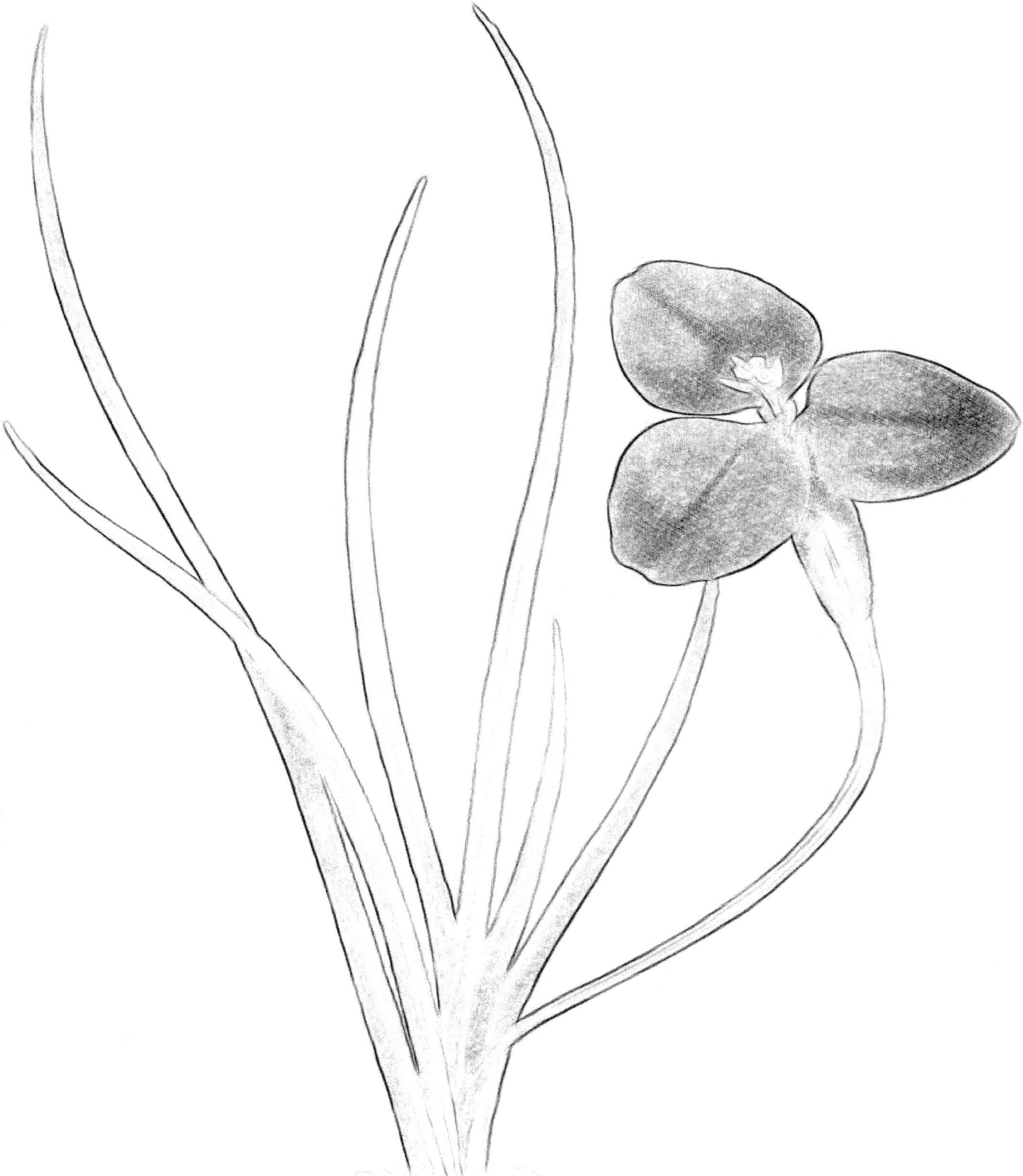

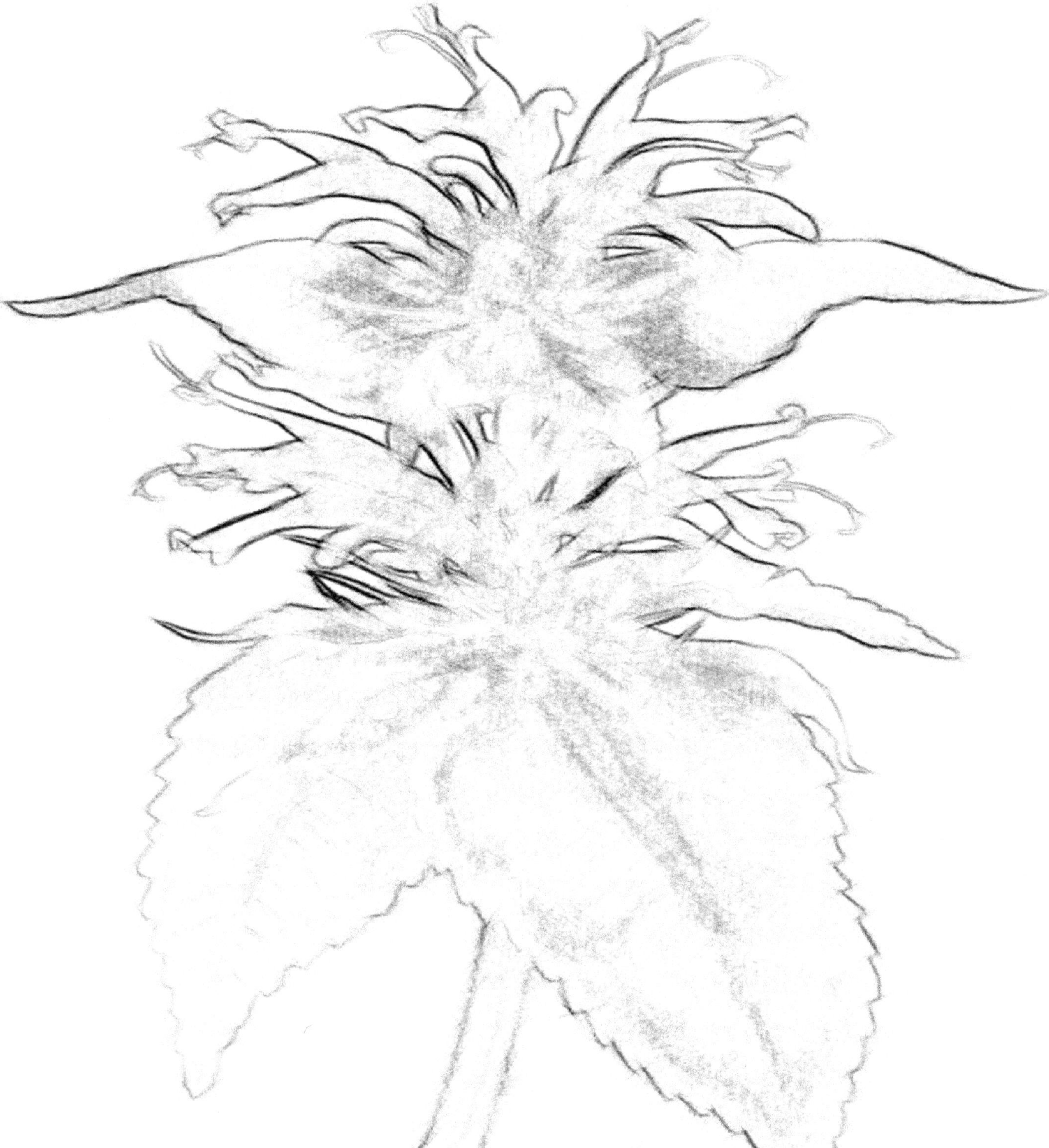

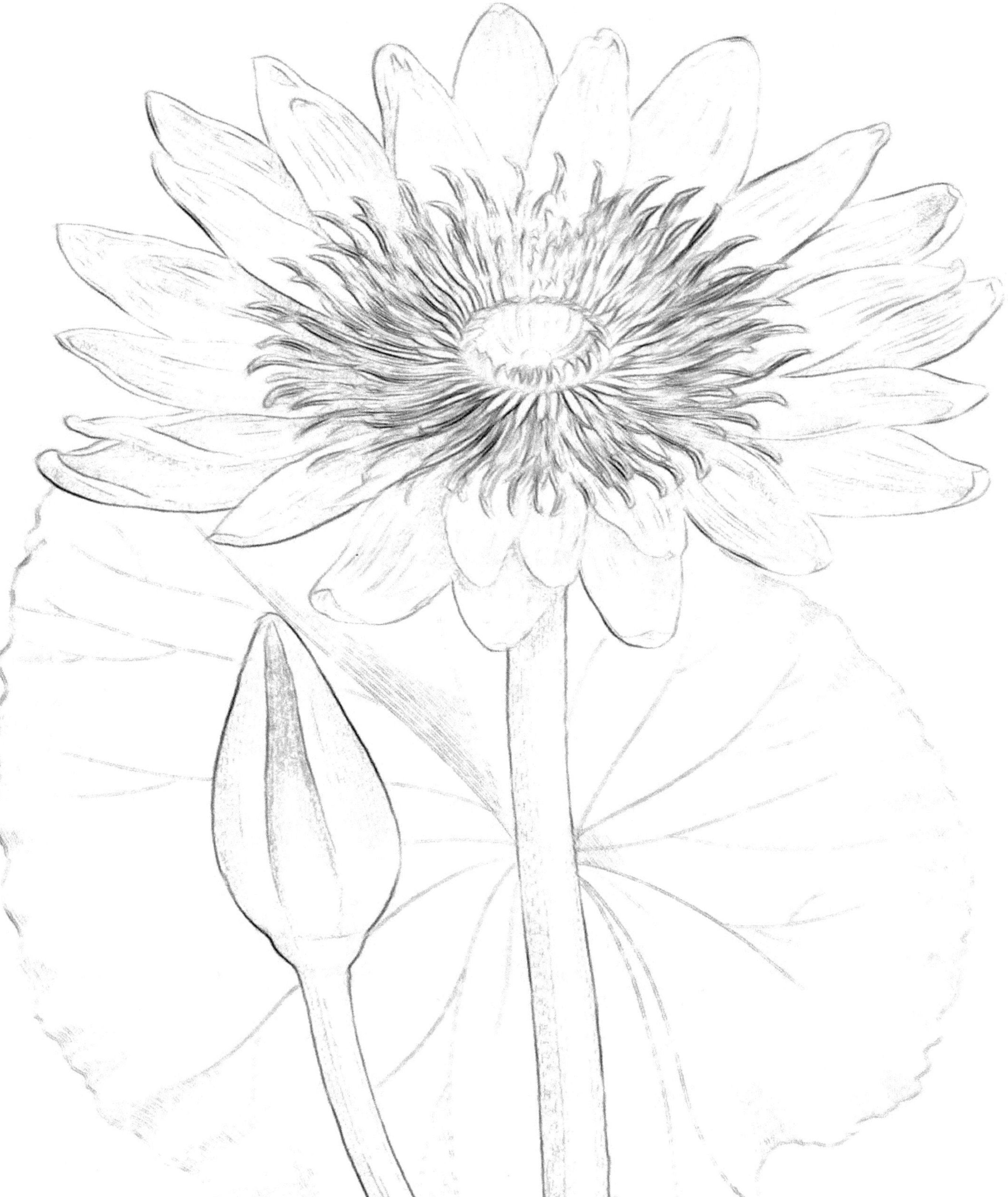

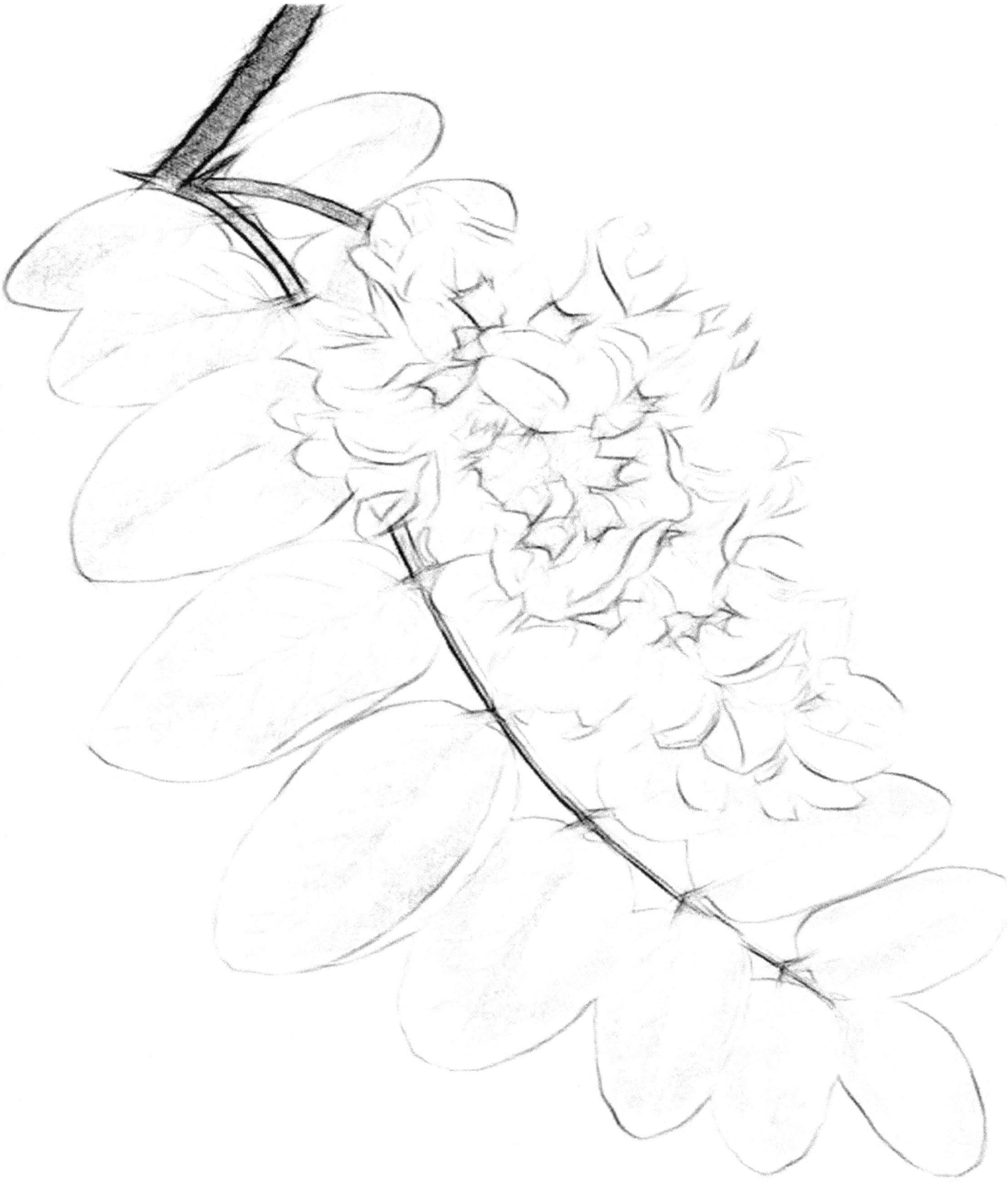

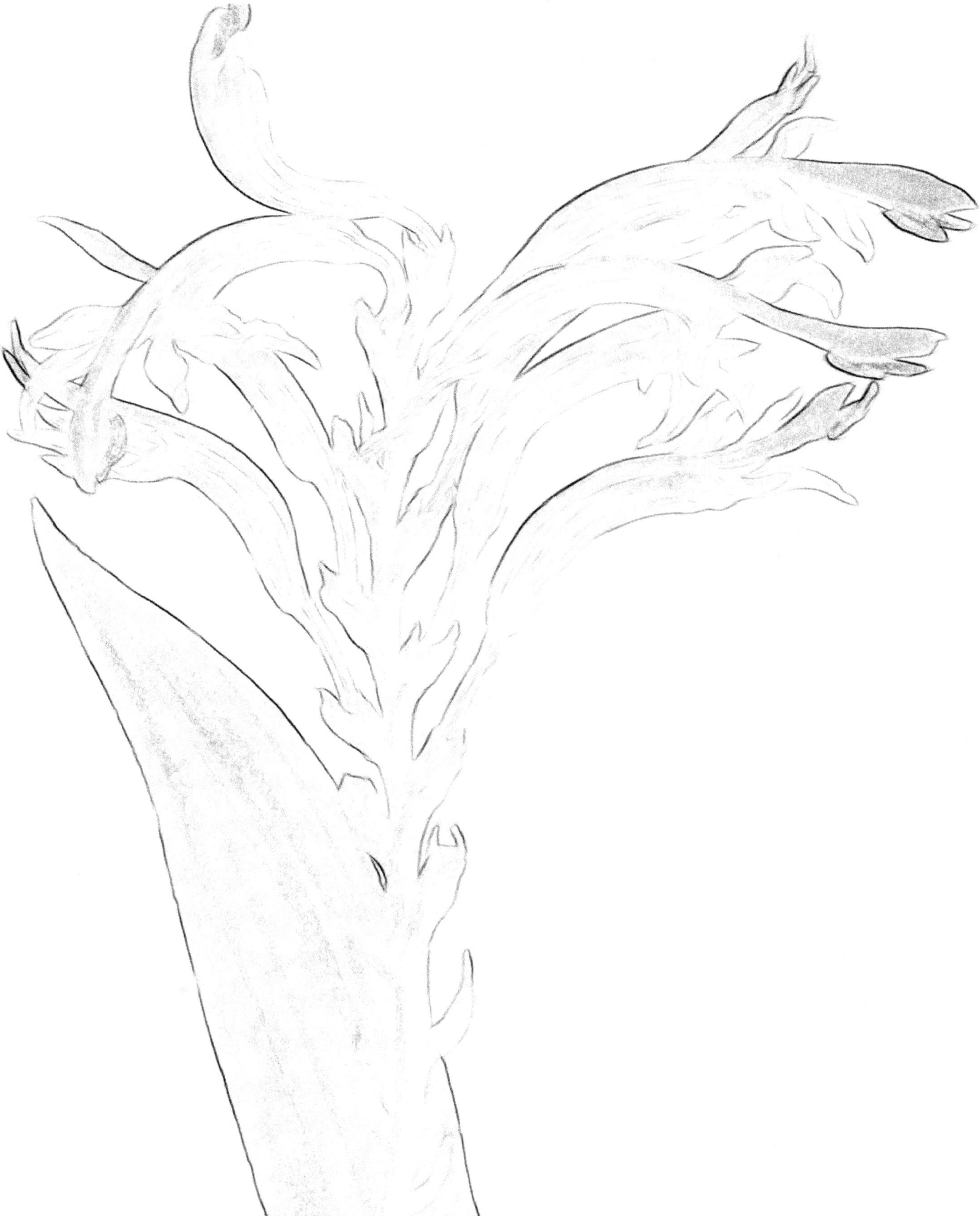

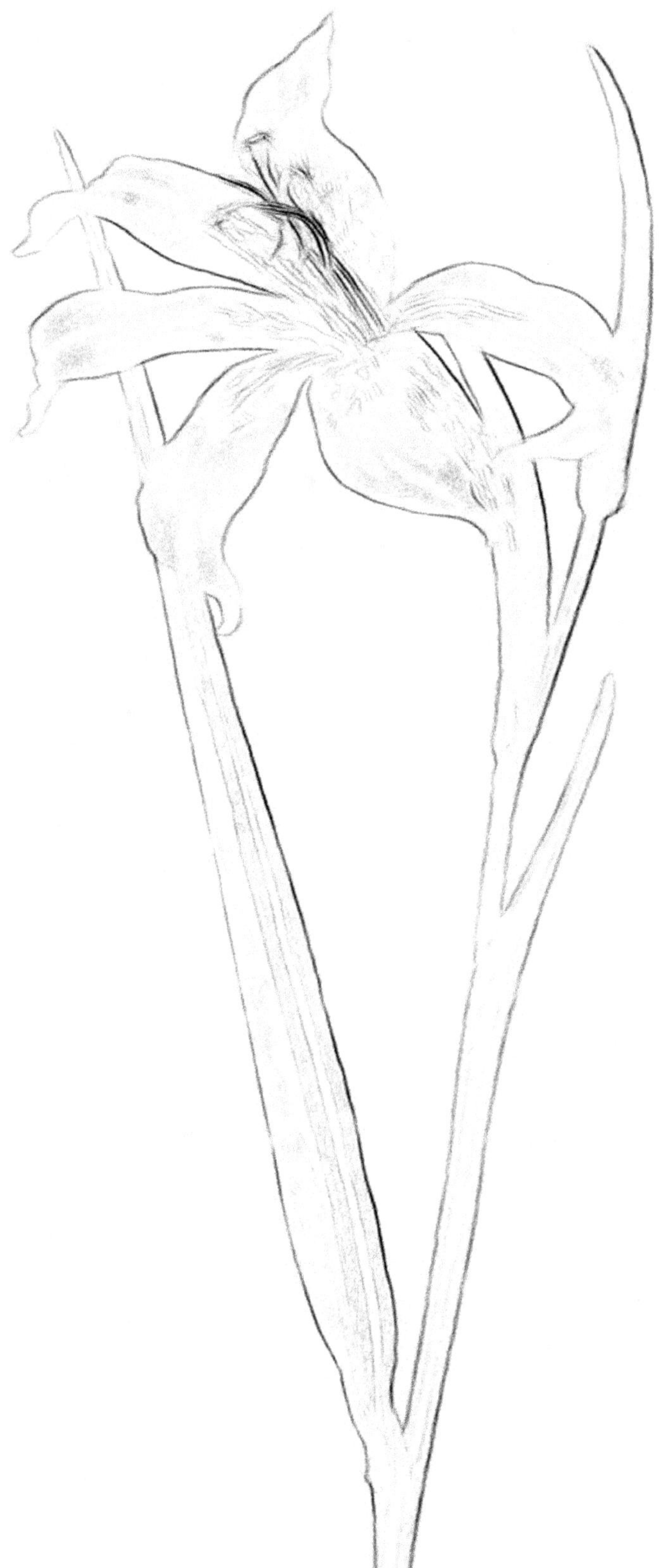

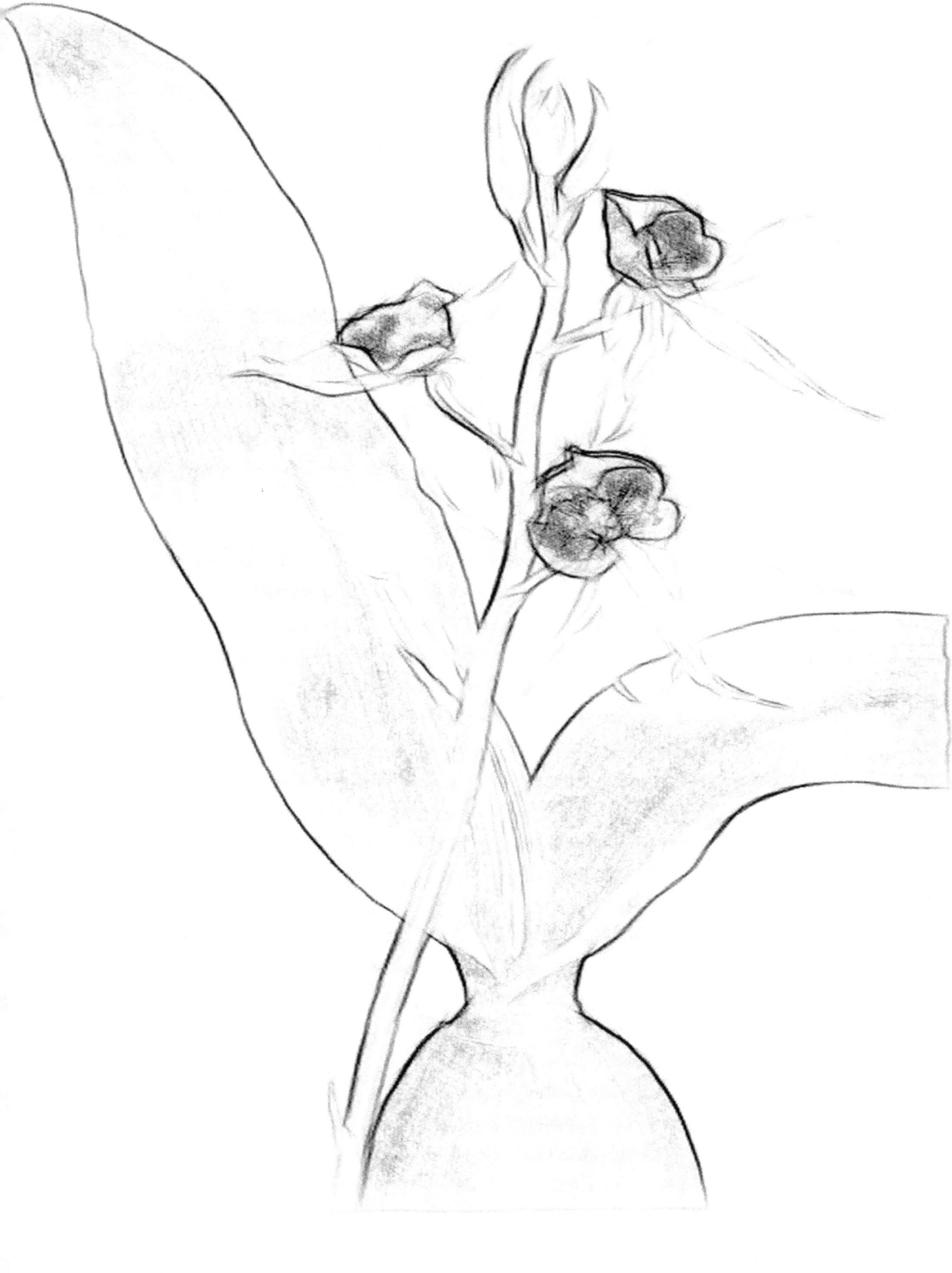

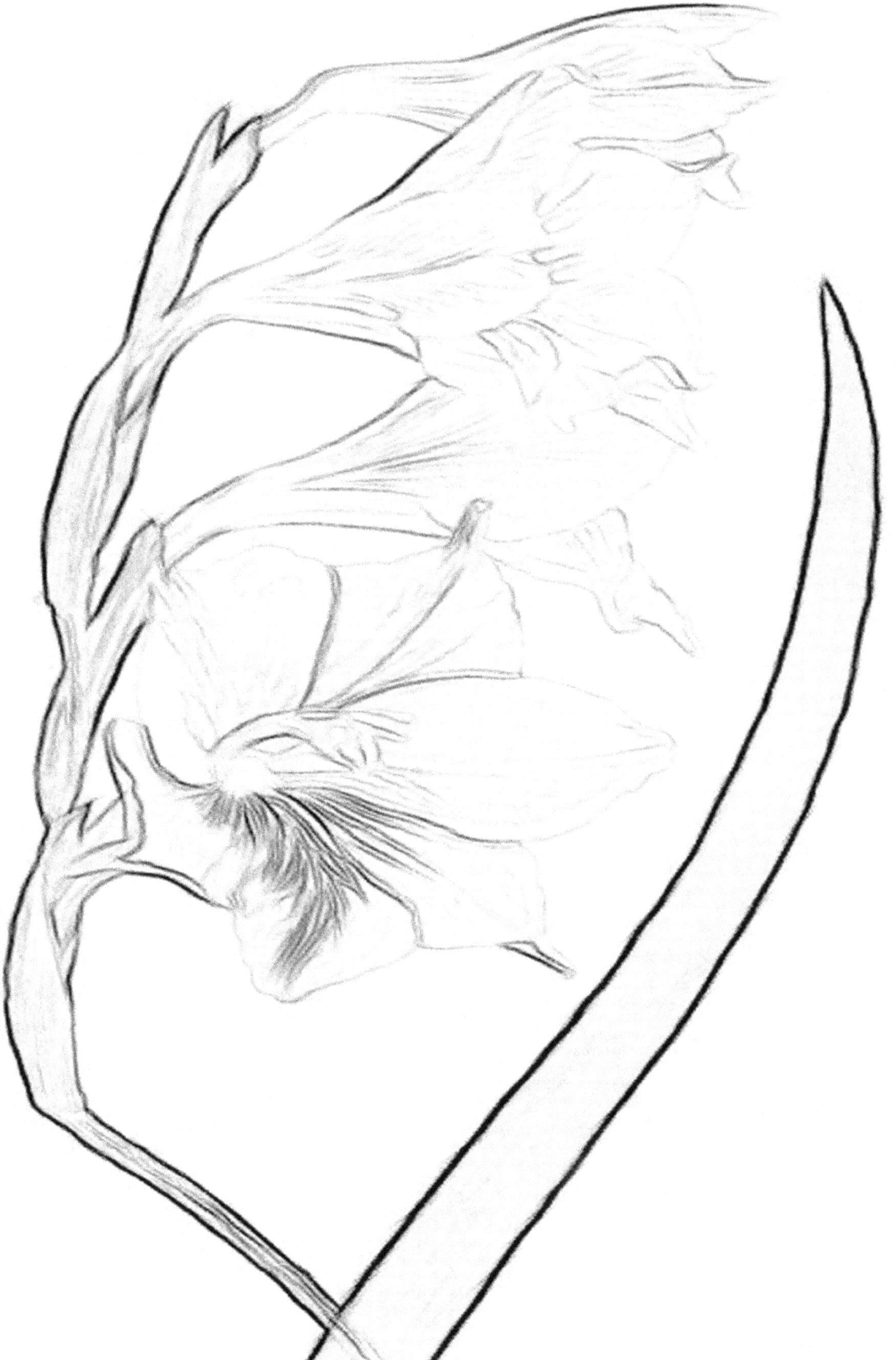

www.ingramcontent.com/pod-product-compliance
Lightning Source LLC
Chambersburg PA
CBHW081305180526
45170CB00007B/2570